Decodable
READER

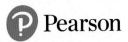

Glenview, Illinois   Boston, Massachusetts
Chandler, Arizona   New York, New York

Pearson Education, Inc. 330 Hudson Street, New York, NY 10013

ISBN-13: 978-0-32-898868-6
ISBN-10: 0-32-898868-5

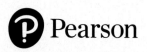

2   18

Unit 3

Unit 4

Unit 5

A Hot Job

Written by Louis Ali

Decodable Reader

1

VC Syllable Pattern

at	bags	big	box	can	fun	get
hot	it	jet	job	less	man	men
net	nuts	rim	sell	top	up	van

High-Frequency Words

away	each	goes	looks	put
than	they	which	with	

The men go up for the nuts
at the top.

It is less fun than it looks.
It is a hot job.

They put the nuts in net bags.
They each put the bags in a
big box.

Which man can get the box?
The box is up to the rim with bags.

Each big box goes in a van.

The van goes to the jet.

The jet takes the nuts away to sell.

Homes

Written by Michael Kwok

Long Vowels CVCe

bike	came	cave	cute	Eve	fine	hike
hole	home	homes	Mike	mile	mine	name
quite	ride	rule	same	tide	time	wide

High-Frequency Words

be	called	here	long
most	one	there	

Homes are not all the same.
There is no rule.
A home can be quite big and wide.

This cute home can sit on a bike.

You can see for a mile in this home!
It is a long hike up.

Most homes do not ride on the tide.
This one can.

My name is Eve.
This home is mine.
I have called it home for a long time.

My name is Mike.
This home is mine.
We just came here.
It will be a fine home for us.

A home can be called a hut, a cave, or a hole.
It can be a home if you are at home there.

A Sound

Written by Maria Garza

Consonant Blends

band	Brad	cluck	drums	flute	grunt	nest
plop	pond	slug	snake	trim	went	

High-Frequency Words

more	move	out	saw
sound	there	things	was

17

Brad went out to the pond to trim
the roses.
There was a sound.

It was not the sound a flute
can make.
It did not sound like a band
with drums.

It was not the sound made when things go plop.

It did not sound like a snake or
a slug.

It did not sound like the grunt
of an ape.

The sound was more like the
cluck of a hen.

Brad saw things move.
Ducks in a nest made the sound!

A Shop by the Path

Written by Jill Baranowski

Consonant Digraphs *ch, ph, sh, wh, th* and Trigraph *-tch*

bench	child	flash	latch	match
path	Phil	phone	shade	shelf
shop	thank	that	thin	things
white	wish			

High-Frequency Words

always	before	find	good	great
means	new	there	warm	work

In the shade of a great elm,
there is a white bench.
The bench is made of thin sticks.

A child can always find a new cape
or cap on a shelf by the white bench.
It is good to be warm.

The bench is by a path that goes past a shop.
The note by the latch means the shop has no phone.

The shop is run by Phil.
He makes things out of cloth
in the shop.

Before Phil goes to work, he
makes a wish.
He would like the cloth to be
cut for him.

In a flash, the cloth is cut in shapes
to match the plans.
Who did that?

The trick is a thank you from the kids for the capes and caps.

My Best Tricks

Written by Lynn Cho

Inflected Ending -s, -es, -ed, -ing

bikes	carries	ending	foxes	glasses
hats	picking	plums	running	saved
slipped	standing	tricks		

High-Frequency Words

come	follow	form	my	of
one	out	show	you	

33

Follow me.
I will show you my best tricks.

I can make foxes come out of hats.
One time the foxes slipped out and
went running around.

I can form a plane out of bikes.
The plane carries my pal and me.

I am picking plums with fun glasses on.

I am standing on a rope.

I will show you my best trick.
I saved it for last.
I can make an ending to this tale.

That is the best trick in my show!

Farm Chores

Written by Andrea Erwin

r-Controlled *ar, or, ore, oar*				Syllables VC/CV	
arm	dark	farm	part	Darling	rabbits
barn	Darling	hard	porch	Darling's	
before	Darling's	horses	roared	kitten	
chores	far	more	sore	Patrick	

High-Frequency Words

before	far	much	went
do	more	this	

41

Patrick went to Jon Darling's farm.
Patrick had not gone
to this farm before.
"Is it far?" Patrick asked.
"Not much more," Mom said.

Patrick spotted Jon's farm.
"His farm has a big red barn!"
Patrick roared.
"Are there horses, mules, and pigs?"
His mom grinned.

Jon Darling sat on his porch
with his kitten.
Patrick jumped out.
Patrick ran up to Jon.

"Are you set to work hard?"
Jon asked.
"We do chores on this farm."
Patrick will do his part
as well as he can.

Patrick swept pens.
Patrick fed chicks and rabbits.
Jon fixed his barn.

Jon Darling stretched his sore back
and patted Patrick's arm.
"You did a nice job," Jon said.

When it got dark,
Patrick went home.
"That was fun!" Patrick said.

Different Snakes

Written by Chi Pham

Decodable Reader

7

Contractions

don't   it's   that's   you've

High-Frequency Words

about	different	know	two	yellow
between	even	look	want	
by	going	people	what	

49

What is different about the
two snakes?
You must look and look.

Don't pet the snakes.
One of them will make you sick
if it bites you.

This snake has red stripes between
black stripes.
It's red by the nose.

That's a king snake.
It's not going to make you sick.

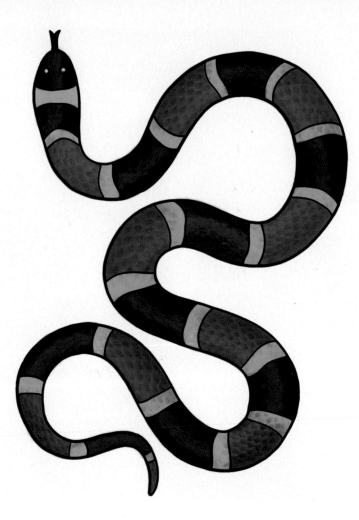

This snake has a black head and red
stripes between yellow stripes.
It's black by the nose.

That's the snake we don't want
around us.
Even a little bite can make you sick.

I hope you've made notes.
Let people know what makes
each snake different.

A Change of Plans

Written by Keesha Barry

Decodable Reader

8

Vowel Digraph _ai_

rain   train

Vowel Digraph _ay_

day   play   rays   stay   way

Vowel Digraph _ea_

great

High-Frequency Words

air	change	her	of	there
are	every	kind	sees	they

57

When she looks up, she sees
a change.
The air is kind of damp.

The rain is on the way.
It's not a great day to go out.

The drops hit her as she makes
her way in.
It's good that she has her rain hat.

She and the kids will play games
and stay in on this day.

She gets the pails set for sand play.
She sets up the train.

The kids play like they are
sending mail.
It is kind of a fun day.

The rays of the sun will be there
the next day.
There is change every day.

Animal Study

Written by Juan Robles

Vowel Digraph *ie*

brief	dried	lie	tie	tried

High-Frequency Words

animal	does	one	out	see	study
are	each	our	point	small	what

We are going to study an animal.
The animal is a fish.
The fish swims in a tank on the shelf.

We will take notes on what we see.
We should make our notes brief and
to the point.

I point out that one fin is big and the other fins are small.

Beth and Luke point out that the fish
does not lie down.
When does it rest?

We tie a snack to a string.
The snack is a dried flake.

We study what the animal does
each day.

Our animal study notes are great!
We tried hard to do a fine job.

My Letter

Written by Mark Hartford

Long e: ee		**Long e: ea**	
creek	queen	each	teach
meet	speech	read	team
needs	week		

		Long e: y	
Long e: ey		Andy	duty
key	valley	army	family
		baby	happy
		Becky	Sandy

High-Frequency Words

about	carry	letter	people
answer	come	others	than
away	every	page	works

This week, each of us at Valley Creek is telling about people with a duty to help others.

Sandy is going to read a page of a speech about the duty of a queen.

Andy is going to teach us about
his family.
They have a duty to meet the needs
of the new baby in the family.

Becky is going to tell that each one on a team has a duty to work hard. The key is to work as a team.

My speech is about my dad.
He works to carry out his duty
far away.
Every day he helps people in need.

I will be happy to answer when
people ask about his job in the army.

My dad can't come see my speech.
But I'm going to send him a letter
to tell him about it.

To the Coast

Written by Cheryl Vilan

Long o: o

go   Jo

Long o: ow

bowl   rows

flow

Long o: oa

boat   goal

coach   loaf

coast   road

float   toast

High-Frequency Words

food   near   people   try

Our team is going to have a sale.
We'll try to make cash to go on
a trip to the coast.

If we go, we will rent a boat so we can float by the coast.

We set up the food tent near
the road.

Each mom and dad cuts a loaf
to make toast.
Coach Jo cracks and cracks
into a bowl.

People start to flow in.
They sit in the rows of seats.
We are near our goal.

The food goes fast.
We met our goal.
We can rent the boat!

Let's go to the coast!

City Goat and Country Goat

Written by Tho Ching

Compound Words

airplane	barnyard	ladybugs
airport	fireworks	tugboat

High-Frequency Words

city	here	said	there
country	lived	school	

89

Once there was a city goat and
a country goat.
The city goat lived by the airport.
"My life isn't so great," said the
city goat.

The country goat lived in a barnyard
by the school.
"My life isn't so great," said the
country goat.

The city goat got on an airplane and
went to the country.

The country goat got on a tugboat
and went to the city.

"There are no fireworks here in
the country.
I need to go home," said the
city goat.

"There are no ladybugs here
in the city.
I miss the school kids.
I need to go home," said the
country goat.

Each goat went home and was
happy to be there.

Earth Every Day

Written by Hai Tran

Long *i: i, ie, y*		Long *i: i_e*		Long *i: igh*	
hi	ties	bikes	pride	high	might
my	Ty	fine	rides	lights	right
pie	why	like	bike		
		miles	time		
		piles			

High-Frequency Words

do	good	thought
Earth	one	would
eyes	others	work

Hi! Earth Day is a fine time to think about our world.
We thought we could do things each week to help the Earth.

My dad rides his bike to work one
time each week.
He bikes for miles.

My mom piles things that can be used one more time.
Why would we put these pie tins by the dump?

Ty ties these up to make a stack as high as he is.

We thought it was good to use
a new light.
It will help our eyes too!
We can shut lights off.

We send letters to ask others
to take pride in our Earth and
do what is right.

I thought you might like to help.
Keep your eyes open for times
you can help the Earth.

The Bravest

Written by Ramona Vargas

Comparative Endings

bigger	bravest	fastest
biggest	deeper	highest
braver	faster	smartest

High-Frequency Words

all	few	know	others
along	head	live	they
away	here	many	what
do	into	move	

I live on the highest piece of ice.
I live here along with many others
like me.
They are all bigger than I am.

They all slide along the trails.
They are all faster than I am.

The others all like to jump off the
biggest rock into the sea.
They are all braver than I am.

I wish to be brave, but the sea is deeper than deep.

A whale comes by.
The others do not know what to do.

I move fast!
I put a few rocks on my head.
I make a big shadow to make the
whale go away.

They say that I am the smartest, fastest, and bravest of all!

The School Paper

Decodable Reader 15

Written by Hannah Johnson

_r_-Controlled Vowel _er_

clerk   Ferndale   ferns   Herb   terms

_r_-Controlled Vowel _ir_

birds   birth   dirt

_r_-Controlled Vowel _ur_

Burt   curb   nurse   turn

High-Frequency Words

about	paper	what
example	something	
have	there	

We have a school paper.
We each get a turn to write
something for the paper.

We use an example from the
Ferndale paper.
This helps us know how to write for
a paper and what terms to use.

Burt and Herb will write about jobs.
Burt will write about his dad, who is
a nurse.

Herb will write about the work that a clerk does in a store each day.

Lee will write about the birth of his baby sis.
Jo will write about one way to plant ferns in the dirt.

I will take a turn.
I'll write about when there was
a nest of birds by the curb.

What is an example of something you could write about for a paper?

Joy's Flowers

Written by Donyette Sanchez

Diphthongs *ou, ow, oi, oy*

brown	how	pound
down	Joy	proud
flower(s)	moist	shower
found	noise	soil
frown	now	sprout
ground	out	without

High-Frequency Words

brown	plant	soil
land	seeds	

121

Joy found a bag of flower seeds.
What can she do with them?
Joy had a frown on her face.
Then she smiled.
She will make a garden in the soil!

122

What will she do first?
Joy will plant her seeds.
A good spot of land
is what Joy needs.

This soil is nice and brown.
Joy digs tiny holes for the seeds.
She will dig holes
for every single one of them!

Now the seeds can be planted.
One seed in each hole
is how it's done.
Put soil on top,
but do not pound it down!

It's time to make the soil moist.
It is a shower for the flowers!
It will help them sprout.
Now they just need sunlight.

When will the flowers sprout?
Without a noise,
the flowers will poke out
of the ground and go up to the sky.

Joy is so proud!
Her flowers did get big.
She will pick one flower
and take it home.

Just for Dad

Written by Jim Martinez

Vowel Team *oo*		**Vowel Team *ue***	
afternoon	foods	blue	glue
bedroom	school	clues	Sue

Vowel Team *ew*		**Vowel Team *ui***	
new	stew	fruit	juice

High-Frequency Words

could	hear	said	something	want
enough	idea	some	they	working

129

Sue and Joy want to do something
kind for Dad.
He is working hard at his new job.
They didn't give him any clues.

That afternoon after school,
they went into the bedroom.
He could not hear them.

Sue has an idea.
They could make some of the foods
he likes.

Joy said that they could make a card
with paper and glue.

They make enough stew
for a crowd.
Sue piles the fruit, and Joy
makes juice.

They put the blue card on the tray
with the food.

"What a great idea!
I can't thank you enough," said Dad.

Book Club

Written by Moshi Chan

Complex Consonant c /s/

city   mice   nice   place   race   space   twice

Complex Consonant g /j/

age   page

Complex Consonant dge /j/

edge   judge

High-Frequency Words

about	book	have	school	what
almost	group	laugh	they	would

137

We have a book club at school.
A group of us meets each day.

The book from last week was about
a boy our age.
He lost an important race.
I checked out that book twice.

The book for this week is about mice
that go to space.
I am almost to the end.
I laugh at every page!

I like a book about a girl and her cat.
They got lost near the edge
of the city.
They had to find a place to get help.

My book club pals judge the best
parts of the book.
We have different ideas almost all
the time.

Our group likes to chat.
We try to be nice and not all speak
at the same time.

What book do you think our group
would like?

Talent Show

Written by Tamara Albertson

Closed Syllables VC/V

closet	model	salad
level	never	talent
limit	River	vanish
magic	Robin	

High-Frequency Words

every	sometimes
from	there
have	young
mountains	

145

It is time for the school talent show.
Every level of young talent will be
on stage.

Robin will do some magic tricks.
The cats will vanish from the closet.
But sometimes the tricks don't work!

Max will bring his young dog, River.
River will go up and down a
pup ramp.

Jess will show her model train set.
The train will go by mountains
and lakes.

Lee will make a salad on stage.
He will never open his eyes while
making it.

Monika is a model.
She will model a dress that she and
her mom made.

Being at camp is just the best!
Sometimes we go on hikes outside.

We are not lazy at camp!
Seth and I say we are not at a hotel.
We hike, swim, and ride.

Sometimes they give a trophy for races.

It is fun to talk with Raven about her pet spider.

Raven named her spider Major.
She put a label on his box.
We could talk for a long time
about Major.

There is a camp song that we
like a lot.
We drink sweet cider and sing.

We think the song is right.
Camp is a super place to be!

The Helpful Gardener

Written by Jan Stroud

Suffixes -ly, -ful, -er, -or, -ish

brightly	hardly	quickly	thankful
closely	helper	selfish	tightly
fondly	helpful	skillful	visitor
gardener	hopeful	sweetly	weekly
gently	peaceful	teacher	

High-Frequency Words

learns	quickly	told
little	teacher	you're

161

"The sun shines brightly,"
Kim said to herself.
Kim's mom is a skillful gardener.
Sunny days are spent helping
Mom in her peaceful garden.

162

Kim is helpful.
She can hardly wait.
She quickly runs
to Mom's garden.
Kim is a good helper.

Kim and her mom work
in the garden weekly.
Kim learns from her mom.
"You're a good teacher,"
Kim told her mom.

164

Mom tends big plants.
Kim tends little plants.
When plants look weak,
Kim gently nurses each plant.

Mom and Kim are hopeful.
This garden is growing well.
"This may be the best garden
we have grown," Mom said,
fondly patting Kim's cheek.
166

Kim hugs her mom tightly.
Then she gets back to her work.
"To be a good gardener like Mom,
I will watch closely and work hard,"
Kim said. "I can't be selfish."

167

Kim smiles sweetly.
She is thankful for this garden.
"Every visitor will like this garden,"
she thought.

In the Woods

Written by Paula Bilika

Prefixes *un-, re-, pre-, dis-*

dislikes	repack	unlocks	unsafe
precooked	unhooks	unpacks	unties
relight	unload	unrolls	

High-Frequency Words

family	night	them
hills	swim	

Kenny and his family
like to go to the woods.
They camp in tents.
They swim in the lake
and hike in the hills.
170

Kenny unlocks the car.
He helps his mom pack.
Dad drives them to a good spot.
Then they unload tents,
full backpacks, and precooked food.

Kenny unties the ropes on the tent.
He helps his mom and dad
set up the tents.
Then Dad unpacks the food
and sets out a yummy dinner.

Kenny likes fishing at the lake.
If Dad gets a tiny fish, he unhooks
it and puts it back in the lake.
Those fish are too little to keep.

Mom puts water on the campfire
when they go hiking.
"It is unsafe to let it burn,"
Mom tells Kenny.
"We can relight it later."
174

At night, Kenny unrolls
his green sleeping bag and slips in.
Sleep will feel good
after his full day
of hiking, fishing, and swimming.

It's time to repack the car.
Kenny dislikes litter,
so he cleans up the campsite.
He doesn't overlook anything.
Kenny can't wait to come back!

176

Chester, the Traffic Horse

Written by Gil Rivera

Syllable Pattern VCCV

basket	plastic
better	reptiles
Chester	summer
costume	traffic
happy	windows
Linda	winter

High-Frequency Words

complete	problem
horse	sometimes
once	their
people	work

Chester is a traffic horse.
Linda is his partner.
They work the streets of the city.

If there is a traffic problem, Chester and Linda will make it better. Sometimes traffic comes to a complete stop.

Once the street was blocked when
a basket of plastic reptiles fell
on the street.

A man in a rabbit costume was a
problem once.
Cars stopped to get a better look.

In winter, Chester and Linda try to keep the snow off of their coats as they work.

In summer, getting too hot can be a problem.

Sometimes people yell, "Thank you!"
out of their car windows.
Chester, the traffic horse, and Linda
are happy to do their jobs.

Meet Tom Lamb

Written by Karen Vincent

Consonant Patterns *kn*, *wr*, *gn*, *mb*

knee	knocking	sign	wrench(es)
kneeled	know	wrapped	wrist
knob	Lamb	wreath	wrong
knocked			

High-Frequency Words

know	truck
man	who

185

An old, white truck
pulled into our driveway.
A man knocked
on our door.

"I know who that is," Dad said.
"It is Tom Lamb.
He has come to fix our pipes."
Dad let the man in.

"What are you making?" Tom asked
as he pulled out his tools.
"It's a flower wreath," I said proudly.
"I made a sign that
has my name too."
188

Tom had his arm wrapped.
My dad asked if he had hurt it.
Tom said that he had hit it
with a wrench.
His wrist was still sore.

Tom had many wrenches.
He kneeled down,
put his knee on the ground,
and then lay under the sink.
Tom turned a knob.

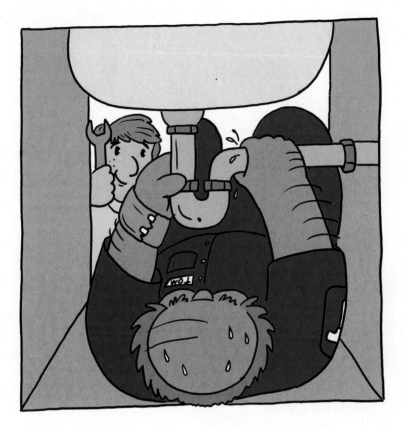

Clink! Clank!
"Oops!" Tom said. "Wrong pipe!"
I held a wrench for Tom
while he looked closer.

When my wreath was done,
I showed Dad and Tom Lamb.
Tom was finished too.
There was no more knocking
in the water pipes.

A Goose in Need

Written by Lauren Delfield

Decodable Reader

25

Homographs

close	left	tears	wound
down	object	wind	

High-Frequency Words

away	said
door	sure
eyes	there
heard	were

We heard the door close.
We were not sure who or what
made it close.
It might just be the wind.

We wound our way down the stairs
to find out.

It was our close pal, Lin.
He was standing by the door with
tears in his eyes.
There were tears on his shirt.

Lin held something close to him in his hands.
"It is stuck, and I sure need your help," he said.

It was an object covered with down.
A little goose had string stuck on its
left wing.
There was no wound or cut.

We needed to help.
We spent time to wind the strings
away from the goose.
The goose did not object.

At last it was free.
We heard the goose honk as it left
with Lin.

Granny Penny

Written by Ricardo Alba

Double Consonants

Anna	cotton	muffins	swimming
attic	Granny	Penny	yellow
buttons	jelly	rabbit	
collects	luggage	summer	

High-Frequency Words

across during there with
become sometimes they

Anna likes to visit Granny Penny
during the summer.
They play in the attic.

Anna puts on costumes that Granny
keeps in luggage up there.
Anna can become a rabbit with a
white tail.

Granny Penny collects buttons that she keeps in cotton bags.

Anna and Granny Penny cook jelly
with fruit they pick.
They like to put jelly across the top
of muffins.

Granny Penny was a swimming
champ at one time.
Her yellow house is across from
the pool.

They go swimming when they
become hot.
Sometimes Granny Penny says,
"Anna, it's time for a splash!"

The best times of all are with Granny
during the summer.

Fun in August

Written by Maggie Yeom

Vowel Patterns *aw, au, au(gh), al*

all	baseball	fall	taller
always	because	falls	thaw
August	caught	launch	walk

High-Frequency Words

best	summer
stop	walk

August is hot!
The sun shines all day.
I cannot stop playing
in the hot, hot sun.

Baseball is the best game
to play in the summer.
We walk or run from base to base.
We always know our team is good.
We win a lot and have fun.

Down at the lake
I caught a fish.
We tried to launch a boat,
but it did not float.
Maybe we'll make a new boat!

212

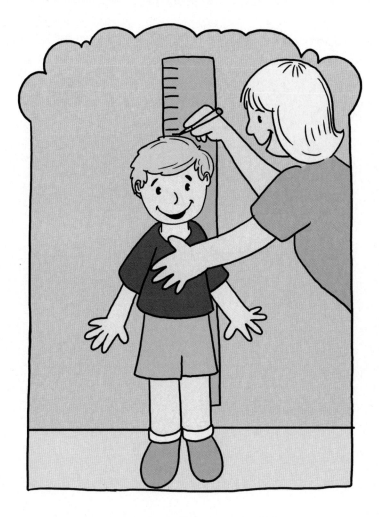

Mom thinks I'm always taller
at the end of a long summer.
I think it's because I run
free on sunny days
through the nice green grass.

213

When August ends,
fall will start.
First, the winds get cooler.
One leaf falls and then more come
down until no leaves are left.

I wait for the cool fall
and cold winter to pass.
I wait for the snow to melt
and the ground to thaw.

Then it happens.
The sun shines longer.
The grass grows again.
Summer is back!
It's time for more fun in the sun.

216

Let's Remember

Decodable Reader

28

Written by Hala Ali

Syllable Pattern VCCCV

complex	pumpkins
contrast	sandwiches
extra	subtract
hundreds	surprise
inspect	

High-Frequency Words

answers	have
are	measure
done	remember
early	some

217

It is no surprise that school will be ending soon.
Let's remember some of the hundreds of things we have done.

We found out how to contrast two
things and tell how they
are different.

In math, we found out how to measure objects and subtract big numbers.

We found out how to inspect complex problems to find answers.

We had fun with pumpkins early in the grade.

We made extra sandwiches for the food bank.

There is so much to remember.
What do you remember most about
this grade?

North Hall Street

Written by Jake Swanson

Abbreviations

Aug.	Mr.	Sat.
Ave.	Mrs.	St.
Dr.	Ms.	

High-Frequency Words

almost   dog   north

A sign said, "Yard Sale on Sat.,
Aug. 17 at 123 North Hall St."
Mr. Walter Hanks saw the sign.
He wrote down the day
and address.

At home, Mr. Hanks told Mrs. Hanks
about the yard sale.
Mr. and Mrs. Hanks planned to go.
Yard sales were great.

Mrs. Hanks took her dog to a vet.
Mrs. Hanks told Dr. Sara Woo
about the sale.
Dr. Woo planned to go.

Dr. Woo told Ms. Nevins.
Hall St. was close to Ms. Nevins'
house on Elm Ave.
She planned on going with her
family.

Mr. and Mrs. Hanks, Dr. Woo, and
Ms. Nevins told more pals.
Almost all of them planned to go
to the sale.
They told other people, too.

On Saturday, Mr. and Mrs. Hanks went to the yard sale at 132 South Hall St.
So did a lot of other people.
But there was no yard sale!

Mr. Hanks looked at his note.
"Whoops, it's not 132, but 123
North Hall St.," he said.
And that is where all the
shoppers went!

Caution!

Written by Mira Lopez

Final Syllable -*le*

little   stable   Uncle

Final Syllable -*sion*

decision   erosion

Final Syllable -*tion*

action   caution   position   solution   station

High-Frequency Words

against   numeral   some
could   people   toward

233

Uncle Ed and Amy walked toward
the little hill.
They could see there was a problem.

The hill was not stable.
Some of the dirt had changed
position.

They made the decision to phone
for help.
Uncle Ed tapped each numeral on
his phone with care.

He called the forest station.
They said they would tackle the
problem and take some action.

Erosion caused the dirt to wash
away.

The man put a caution sign against the big tree.

This could be a good solution to keep people safe.